Clara Barton

by Lola M. Schaefer

Consulting Editor: Gail Saunders-Smith, Ph.D.

Consultants: The Staff of the
Clara Barton National Historical Site
Glen Echo, Maryland

Pebble Books

an imprint of Capstone Press
Mankato, Minnesota

Pebble Books are published by Capstone Press
151 Good Counsel Drive, P.O. Box 669, Mankato, Minnesota 56002
http://www.capstone-press.com

Library of Congress Cataloging-in-Publication Data
Schaefer, Lola M., 1950–
    Clara Barton / by Lola M. Schaefer.
    p. cm.—(First biographies)
    Summary: Simple text and photographs present the life of Clara Barton, who
worked as a nurse during the Civil War and founded the American Red Cross
Society in 1881 to help people hurt by war or disasters.
    Includes bibliographical references and index.
    ISBN 0-7368-1434-5 (hardcover)
    ISBN 0-7368-9410-1 (paperback)
    1. Barton, Clara, 1821–1912—Juvenile literature. 2. Red Cross—United States—
Biography—Juvenile literature. 3. Nurses—United States—Biography—Juvenile
literature. [1. Barton, Clara, 1821-1912. 2. Nurses. 3. Women—Biography.]
I. Title. II. Series.
HV569.B3 .S33 2003
361.7′634′092—dc21   2002001216

Note to Parents and Teachers

The First Biographies series supports national history standards for units on people and culture. This book describes and illustrates the life of Clara Barton. The photographs support early readers in understanding the text. This book also introduces early readers to subject-specific vocabulary words, which are defined in the Words to Know section. Early readers may need assistance to read some words and to use the Table of Contents, Words to Know, Read More, Internet Sites, and Index/Word List sections of the book.

Table of Contents

Young Clara 5

Helping Soldiers 13

American Red Cross 19

Words to Know 22

Read More 23

Internet Sites 23

Index/Word List 24

Time Line

1821
born

Clara Barton was born in Massachusetts in 1821. She had two older brothers and two older sisters.

birthplace of Clara Barton in North Oxford, Massachusetts

Time Line

1821
born

1833–1835
takes care of
brother David

Clara's brother David was hurt badly in a fall. Clara took care of him for two years until he was better.

Clara's brother David grew up to be a soldier.

Time Line

1821
born

1833–1835
takes care of
brother David

1839
becomes a
teacher

Clara became a teacher. She taught in a one-room schoolhouse. She liked teaching. Clara taught for 13 years.

Time Line

1821 born	1833–1835 takes care of brother David	1839 becomes a teacher	1860 moves to Washington, D.C.

10

In 1860, Clara moved to Washington, D.C. Soon, the Civil War began. Clara knew that soldiers needed food, clothing, and other supplies. She wanted to help.

 Washington, D.C., around 1860

1861
Civil War
begins

Time Line

1821
born

1833–1835
takes care of
brother David

1839
becomes a
teacher

1860
moves to
Washington, D.C.

Clara wrote to newspapers. She asked people to send supplies for the soldiers. Next, she asked to visit the battlefields to bring supplies to the soldiers.

1861
Civil War
begins

W.M. Allison

Time Line

| 1821 born | 1833–1835 takes care of brother David | 1839 becomes a teacher | 1860 moves to Washington, D.C. |

Clara helped hurt soldiers on the battlefields. She fed them and fixed their wounds. She was kind to them. Soldiers called Clara the "Angel of the Battlefield."

1861
Civil War
begins

1862
begins visiting
battlefields

Time Line

1821
born

1833–1835
takes care of
brother David

1839
becomes a
teacher

1860
moves to
Washington, D.C.

After the war, many soldiers were missing. Clara helped families find about 22,000 missing or dead soldiers.

1861
Civil War
begins

1862
begins visiting
battlefields

American
Red Cross

Time Line

1821	1833–1835	1839	1860
born	takes care of	becomes a	moves to
	brother David	teacher	Washington, D.C.

In 1881, Clara created the American Red Cross Society. This group helps people hurt by war or disasters. It gives them supplies, food, and the help they need to get better.

◀ American Red Cross Society headquarters in Glen Echo, Maryland

1861	1862	1881
Civil War begins	begins visiting battlefields	creates American Red Cross Society

Time Line

| 1821 born | 1833–1835 takes care of brother David | 1839 becomes a teacher | 1860 moves to Washington, D.C. |

Clara Barton died in 1912. Today, the American Red Cross still helps people hurt by war or disasters.

1861	1862	1881	1912
Civil War begins	begins visiting battlefields	creates American Red Cross Society	dies

Words to Know

American Red Cross Society—an organization that helps people hurt by disasters, such as floods, earthquakes, fires, or war; Clara Barton created the American Red Cross Society in 1881.

battlefield—the ground where soldiers fight

Civil War—the U.S. war between the Northern states and the Southern states; the Civil War was fought from 1861 to 1865.

disaster—an event that causes great damage, loss, or suffering; disasters include floods, tornados, fires, and wars.

soldier—someone who is in the military

supplies—materials needed to do something; Clara gathered supplies such as bandages, soap, and food for Civil War soldiers.

wound—an injury or cut

Read More

Ruffin, Francis E. *Clara Barton.* American Legends. New York: PowerKids Press, 2002.

Wheeler, Jill C. *Clara Barton.* Portraits of Inspiration. Minneapolis: Abdo Publishing, 2002.

Woodworth, Deborah. *Compassion: The Story of Clara Barton.* Plymouth, Minn.: Child's World, 1998.

Internet Sites

Clara Barton
http://www.galegroup.com/free_resources/whm/bio/barton_c.htm

Clara Barton, 1821–1912
http://www.americancivilwar.com/women/cb.html

Clara Barton National Historic Site
http://www.nps.gov/clba

Index/Word List

American Red Cross Society, 19, 21
Barton, David (brother), 7
battlefield, 13, 15
born, 5
brother, 5, 7
Civil War, 11
dead, 17
died, 21
disaster, 19, 21
help, 11, 15, 17, 19, 21
hurt, 7, 15, 19, 21
Massachusetts, 5
missing, 17
newspapers, 13
people, 13, 19, 21
schoolhouse, 9
sisters, 5
soldiers, 11, 13, 15, 17
supplies, 11, 13, 19
teacher, 9
visit, 13
war, 17, 19, 21
Washington, D.C., 11
wounds, 15

Word Count: 201
Early-Intervention Level: 22

Editorial Credits

Martha E. H. Rustad, editor; Heather Kindseth, series designer; Linda Clavel, illustrator; Patrick Dentinger, book designer; Wanda Winch, photo researcher; Karen Risch, product planning editor

Photo Credits

American Red Cross, 18 (inset)
Clara Barton National Historic Site, National Park Service, cover, 1, 4, 6, 8, 16 (both), 18, 20
Corbis, 10, 12
Library of Congress/William M. Allison, 14